Beyond the Rainbow

Beyond the Rainbow

A Workbook for Children
in the Advanced Stages of a Very Serious Illness

Written by Marge Eaton Heegaard

To be illustrated by children

Fairview Press, Minneapolis

Published by Fairview Press, 2450 Riverside Avenue, Minneapolis, Minnesota 55454-1400. Fairview Press is a division of Fairview Health Services, a community-focused health system providing a complete range of services, from the prevention of illness and injury to care for the most complex medical conditions. For a free current catalog of Fairview Press titles, please call toll-free 1-800-544-8207. Or visit our Web site at www.fairviewpress.org.

First Printing: January 2003

Printed in Canada
06 05 04 03   6 5 4 3 2 1

Cover by Laurie Ingram Design, www.laurieingramdesign.com
Interior by Dorie McClelland, Spring Book Design

Funding and support for *Beyond the Rainbow* provided by Deva House.

We gratefully acknowledge the following experts for their assistance:
  Harriet Kohen, LICSW; Jason Albrecht, child-family life specialist; Kris Frey, child-family life specialist; Stacy Stickney Ferguson, LICSW; and Janet Ziegler, LGSW, of Fairview-University Medical Center in Minneapolis, Minnesota.
  Gwen Feather, RN, MS, CHPN; Wayne Leaver, LMHC; Rachel Friesen, LCSW; Michele Meyer, MA; and W. Chien, MD, of Hope Hospice in Fort Meyers, Florida.
  Bruce Himelstein, MD, of Children's Hospital of Wisconsin in Milwaukee.
  Eric Stephanson of Canuck Place Children's Hospice in Vancouver, British Columbia.
  Warren Anderson of St. Mary's Hospital in Rochester, Minnesota.

A message for parents and other adults

This book is designed for children (ages six through twelve) in the advanced stage of a serious illness. They may illustrate this book with pictures they choose to draw. The pages in the book not only will help families communicate, but allow adults to evaluate children's understanding and feelings about their illness.

Children are more often able to share difficult concerns with pictures rather than words. While young children may need help understanding some of the words and concepts in this book, adults should encourage them to make their own decisions about what to draw or write. This provides a sense of empowerment.

Give each child a small box of new crayons to illustrate the book. While many children enjoy drawing with markers, crayons often encourage greater self-expression. Older children might prefer to use colored pencils and may add more words.

The art process allows a child to symbolically express sadness, fear, anger, and anxiety. Periodically invite the child to tell you more about his or her work, focusing on expression rather than artistic technique. As children learn to understand and communicate their feelings, they will develop important coping skills. Do not try to protect children from difficult feelings. Research shows that both children and adults do better if they share their concerns. If a drawing reveals a misconception, gently correct the child. Remember, what a child perceives is as powerful as reality.

Adults can help children cope

It is natural to want to shield children, but research shows that children do better if they have open and honest communication about their illness. Most children are aware of their condition even when the truth has been hidden from them. In fact, they may conceal their own knowledge to protect the adults around them. Hiding feelings increases anxiety and builds walls in a relationship, preventing the love, comfort, and honest communication that children need. Without open and honest communication, children feel isolated.

Honesty does not mean overloading children with information beyond their years. It means being truthful and sharing feelings. This helps both children and adults grow stronger and closer. Children can learn that they do not have to face life's most difficult task alone.

Children need an accepting environment so they can express resentment and disappointment. They are often scared and feel picked on. Fear of illness and death may be constantly on their mind. Artwork allows them to share their inner thoughts with people who care about them.

Younger children may believe that their illness is a punishment for something they did or did not do. They need reassurance that their illness is no one's fault and that no one wants to hurt them, even though helping sometimes does hurt.

Because children will often try to protect adults, they may not want others to see them cry. It is important for adults to express their own sadness, teaching children that crying can release sad emotions and help people feel better.

Some children need to deny their feelings to cope, but many children are able to share their feelings about death. While they may see it as the end of life in this world, they often believe in a spirit or soul that lives on. Adults should try to respect children's beliefs about the mysteries of mortality.

By living as fully as possible, seriously ill children may gain a maturity beyond their years. They often leave a legacy of strength, determination, and greater appreciation for life and relationships.

This book is intended to help children:

To children

This is a book to help you understand and express thoughts and feelings that often seem too difficult for words. This is your book, and you can make your own decisions about what to draw or write in it. You will make it special from all other books by drawing your own pictures or writing your own poems. If you have trouble understanding any words in this book, ask an adult to help you.

You do not need any special skills to draw or write on the pages. Just use lines, shapes, and colors to draw pictures that come into your mind as you read the words on each page. Sometimes you may choose to write a poem to express what you are thinking or feeling.

Do the pages in order, beginning with the first page. You may skip any pages that feel uncomfortable, but you may want to go back and work on them another day. When you have done a few pages, stop and share your work with someone who cares about you.

You will feel better when you are able to share your thoughts and feelings with others.

The sky above is always changing. Sunshine disappears into clouds. Rain falls. Sometimes a rainbow appears.

(Draw a changing sky.)

Our world is always changing. It is easy to see changes in the sky above.

The world below also changes. Seasons change. Weather changes. Trees change.

(Draw a change in nature.)

Change is a natural part of life and growth.

People change, too. I have changed from being healthy to being very sick. I have a very serious illness. It is called _____ and my life has changed.

(Draw some changes in your life caused by your illness.)

Change can bring many different feelings and thoughts.

I remember when I first got sick. I wondered why it happened to me. Sometimes I tried to pretend nothing was different.

(Draw a picture of what you first thought and felt about your illness.)

Nothing you did made you sick. No one picked you to get sick. Illness just happens.

I know some things about my illness, but I still have questions.

(List things you know in the first column, questions in the second.)

Things I Know	Questions I Have

It is O.K. to ask adults for answers to your questions.

I have had many medicines and treatments. I do not like some of them!
(Draw a picture of what you do not like.)

Treatments sometimes hurt. It is O.K. to ask questions about your medicines and treatments. You might even ask how to make them less scary or painful.

Because of this illness, I have learned something important about myself.
(Draw a picture or write a poem about it.)

Sometimes, something good can come from bad times.

A PICTURE FROM ME

(Draw the first letters of your first and last names—BIG.
Add lines and colors to turn them into a picture.)

You can make lots of pictures this way!

I have many feelings that I feel in my body.

(Close your eyes and think of a time you had a strong feeling. Choose a color to show where you feel that feeling in your body. Scribble the color next to the correct word below.)

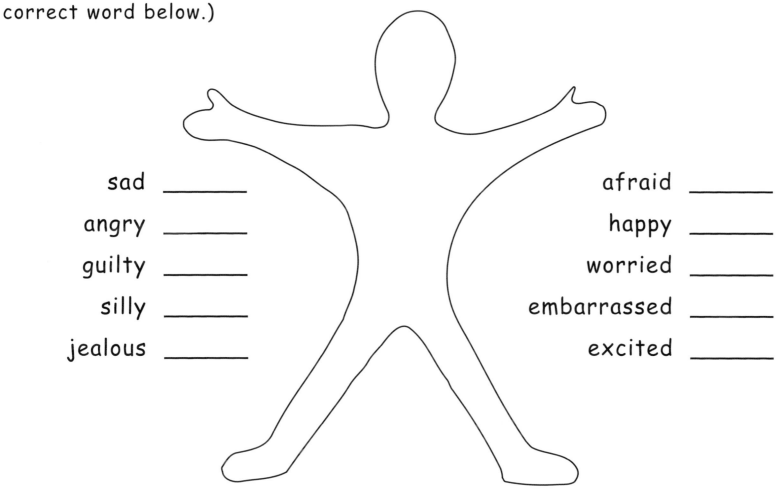

sad _____

angry _____

guilty _____

silly _____

jealous _____

afraid _____

happy _____

worried _____

embarrassed _____

excited _____

All feelings are O.K. Feelings change.

Sometimes I feel very angry.

(Draw an angry time. Show how you let others know that you were angry.)

Feeling angry is O.K. It is <u>not</u> O.K. to hurt people or things. It is O.K. to use words or draw pictures to let others know how you feel.

There are times I feel sad.

(Draw a sad time. Show how you let others know that you were sad.)

It is O.K. to cry and let sadness out. Sharing sadness with others can help people feel better.

I am afraid sometimes.

(Draw what you are afraid of.)

You can tell people what scares you and what they can do to make it better. How do you let others know you are afraid?

When I am afraid, I can pretend I am something else to help me feel strong or safe.

(Draw a mask you could put on to pretend to be something else.)

You can make choices when you are afraid.

I have courage.

(Draw a time you were brave.)

Courage is feeling brave and trying something new or difficult.

My illness causes pain in my body.

(Choose one color and scribble that color on the places that hurt.)

It is important to tell someone when and where you hurt. Who do you tell?

GAINING POWER OVER PAIN

(Try these exercises.)

1. Close your eyes and see your pain. Give it a shape, size, and color. Now, imagine something you can send to the places you hurt to drive the pain away. Watch your pain change color, shape, and size until you feel better.

2. Imagine your body all relaxed like a soft toy. Breathe in and out very slowly and deeply. Give love a special color and send it through your body until you feel better.

3. Imagine your body all relaxed like a soft toy. Breathe in and out very slowly and deeply. Pretend your pain is something outside your body and watch it go away.

As you practice these exercises, they will get easier to do.

16

FREE CHOICE PICTURE

(Draw or write anything you choose.)

You are in charge of this page!

I need and want comfort.

(Draw a picture of the way you like to be comforted.)

You can close your eyes and imagine being comforted like that now.

I have people to whom I can tell important things.

(Draw a picture of one or more of these people.)

You can choose what, when, and with whom you want to share.

People find it hard to talk about some things.
(Draw an X by the words that are most true for you.)

I can share all of my feelings:

   easily and often _____   sometimes _____   not often _____

Things that are hard for me to talk about are:

   my illness _____   feelings _____   dying _____   other _____

I am:

   sick _____   very sick _____   dying _____   scared _____

   hopeful _____   peaceful _____   other _____

I think about death:

sometimes _____ all the time _____ never _____

I would like to talk about dying to:

Mom _____ Dad _____ brother _____ sister _____

friend _____ doctor _____ grandparent _____

rabbi, priest, or pastor _____ other _____

When people die, I think:

they go to heaven _____ come back in a new form _____

become part of those they love _____ other _____

When people can talk more about death, it becomes less scary.

Many people have trouble talking about death, but death is part of life. (Draw a picture or write a poem called "Death.")

Drawing a picture or writing a poem may be easier than talking about it.

All living things die sometime. Death is not like sleeping. It is the end of seeing, feeling, breathing, and doing. It is also the end of pain and suffering. When we die, we live on in different ways. Many people wonder what lies beyond the rainbow. What do you believe?

(Draw a picture or write a poem.)

During their lives, people bring joy and love to others in a way that will always be remembered.

If I were ever to die, I hope someone would use or take care of my favorite things.

(List or draw a picture of your special things and who you would give them to.)

People live on in the memories of loved ones and in the things they leave behind.

There are some special things I would like to say to special people.

(Write a letter to someone.)

It is important to let others know how you feel about them.

I am special and hope to be remembered in a special way.
(Write a poem or a few words about the ways you are special.)

Your illness has given you strength to face very difficult problems. You have touched the hearts and minds of those around you. You are special and will not be forgotten.

It is O.K. to make a wish.

(Draw a picture or use words to describe your wish.)

Each day is a new beginning. Wishes can come true. Beyond the rainbow there is a bright light shining with hope for you!

Also available from Fairview Press

Cuando alguien muy especial muere: Los niños pueden aprender a enfrenar la adversidad, by Marge Eaton Heegaard. The Spanish edition of *When Someone Very Special Dies: Children Can Learn to Cope with Grief*. The world's bestselling art therapy book for grieving children, this book teaches basic concepts of death, helping kids to understand and express the many feelings they have when a loved one dies.

Saying Goodbye to Your Pet: Children Can Learn to Cope with Pet Loss, by Marge Eaton Heegaard. An art therapy book for children coping with the loss of a pet, *Saying Goodbye to Your Pet* offers sensitive exercises to help children say in pictures what they are unable to say in words. The completed book serves as a lasting keepsake, honoring the memory of the family pet and its importance in the child's life.

Drawing Together to Develop Self-Control, by Marge Eaton Heegaard. An art therapy book for children with controllable behavioral problems. *Drawing Together to Develop Self-Control* helps kids learn the consequences of their actions, how their behavior affects others, how to develop good judgment skills, and more.

For more information, call 1-800-544-8207, visit our Web site at www.fairviewpress.org,
or write to Fairview Press, 2450 Riverside Avenue, Minneapolis, MN 55454